My Prudent Advice

LESSONS FOR MY DAUGHTER

by
JAIME MORRISON CURTIS

CHRONICLE BOOKS

SAN FRANCISCO

ISBN 978-1-4521-0783-7

Manufactured in China
Design by Jennifer Tolo Pierce
Illustrations by Lydia Ortiz
Typeset in Bodoni Egyptian and Whitney

5 7 9 10 8 6 4

Chronicle Books LLC
680 Second Street
San Francisco, CA 94107
www.chroniclebooks.com

My child, if as a baby you were sometimes comforted by my loving care, and if your heart preserves the memory of those moments, I hope you will place your trust in this advice, which is prompted by my love for you, and that it will help you to be happy.

— **ADVICE TO MY DAUGHTER (1794)** Marie Jean Antoine Nicolas de Caritat, Marquis de Condorcet

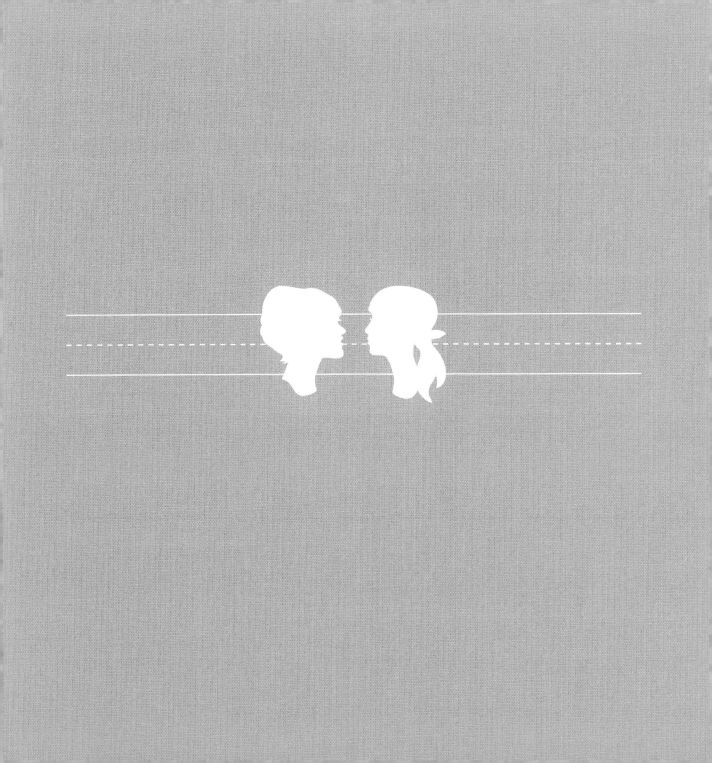

Contents

This Is for You

F ew things are quite as intimidating as a blank sheet of paper, but even
fewer things as satisfying as filling it up. The apprehension and reward
are not unlike the work of raising a child. Like a newborn baby, the page is
fresh, clean, and utterly powerless over the story about to unfold; ready to be
filled with thoughts of your choosing; at the mercy of the time and attention
you give it. There is something charmingly old-fashioned about keeping a
journal—it's much like quilted receiving blankets, heirloom baby dresses,
and family recipes shared over Thanksgiving dinner. When your world turns
upside down, as often happens with a baby's arrival, these simple pleasures
can feel like anchors to past mothers on your family tree, keeping you steady
as you find your own way. When your head and heart are adrift in a storm
of love, exhaustion, and overwhelming expectation, falling back on the

tried-and-true process of writing may be the only way to regain your balance; your words will surely become a timeworn treasure for future women of your family. This is an invitation to contemplate your legacy to your children and to share it. Write for yourself, and write for your daughter. Fill these pages with the love and consideration you both deserve. I believe that is a worthy effort that will reward both generations. By having access to this assembled wisdom, girls will know the depth of consideration and love they were given and, as a result, will have a solid springboard into their own independent lives, as well as a soft place to land at home. While what it means to be a girl may alter by the decade, some things never change. A mother's love goes on forever.

On Your Beginnings

It is a special gift to understand where you came from, who your parents are, and what your birth meant to your family. I hope to paint you a picture of what our life together is like now; perhaps one day it will help you figure out where you're going.

I am your mother. My name is ....

....

I was .... *years old the day you were born.*

You were born at: ....

....

We live:

....

....

....

I chose to name you .... *because:*

....

....

....

I learned you were a girl when:

....

....

....

....

My reaction to the news was:

....

....

....

....

....

I have decided to write this journal for you because:

....

....

....

....

....

I hope that when you read it, you feel:

....

....

....

....

....

On Family

Family is a finicky beast—the only living thing that you don't choose and can't escape. Right now you are a fuzzy cub we huddle together to protect. Perhaps your skin cells will retain a memory of the warmth of our touch and provide you with a sense of security as you age, so that you may never feel the drought of alienation. As your personality reveals itself, you may at times feel like a black sheep, but let me assure you every family is an assortment of odd ducks. As you grow, you will encounter obstacles inconceivable to you now, and your circle of kin will help you face them with grace. The sense of obligation this puts on you may strike you alternately as a blessing and a curse. Let me tell you without reservation that your duty to this family, and our reciprocal bind to you, is a blessing, so that you may never feel abandoned. You are not, and never will be, alone in this world. These are my thoughts on honoring your familial ties as an adult, as we have embraced you as a child.

About my mother:

....

....

....

....

....

....

Create a sense of family wherever you are.
Find people to love, and love them unconditionally.

About my father:

....

....

....

....

....

....

About my siblings:

....

....

....

....

....

....

....

Come home.

Don't stay away from home for too long, if only because my heart breaks
a little every week we spend apart.

The three words that best describe my childhood are:

....

....

....

Take snapshots.

I mean this both literally and figuratively. Browsing old family photos is such a rare comfort—a few unbounded moments flipping through two-dimensional treasures, feeling connected to a group of people unknown and long gone—that you owe it to future daughters to contribute to the visual record of your generation. But I also want you to learn to take mental snapshots as an exercise in appreciating your life as it is right now. Pressing a pause button while the action swells around you doesn't require any fancy equipment, yet the memories you forge will be the sumptuous reward of your old age. Stop briefly to notice the loveliness of a scene—how the air smells, the lilt of voices—and record it for yourself alone, so that you may play it back in your mind as long as your faculties allow. Then happiness will always be at your fingertips.

A challenge we faced as a family:

....

....

....

....

....

If you love someone, tell them.
And tell them often. It's a wonderful feeling to be reminded that you are loved.

Some values I believe our family shares:

....

....

....

....

....

....

Children are wonderful, but you don't have to have them.

Having a child felt like an imperative to me, and I'm so glad it did because you arrived. But I want you to know that you don't need to become a mother to be a full and complete woman. I promise not to beg you for grandchildren (no, I don't).

My hope is that when you think of home as an adult you feel:

....

....

....

....

....

 Remember family birthdays.

Write them down somewhere or program them into your robot or whatever you have to do. They'll be really sad if you forget.

Some wisdom passed down through our family . . .

My mother would always say:

....

....

....

....

....

....

....

My father would always say:

....

....

....

....

....

....

....

More prudent advice

On Friendship

As you become more independent, your sphere of relationships will expand beyond your family into the wilderness of friendship. You will develop affections that change you, uplift you, and even occasionally abandon you. While it is expected that you be considerate to everyone, it is also wise to be selective with whom you develop deeper intimacy. Building a strong friendship is a delicate dance, with dips and spins that can both elevate and hurt, more than twisted ankles ever could. A real ally offers support, sincerity, and blistering honesty borne of love. Don't allow yourself, or any friend of yours, to neglect the responsibility of candid communication, buffered with sincere consideration and thoughtful choice of words and deeds. This kind of frank familiarity is the mark of a true friend, the love of which is essential to feeling understood, known, and less alone in the world.

My oldest friend:

....

....

....

....

If you test people, they may fail.
Friendship, love, and family don't hinge on any single success or failure; you would do yourself a disservice to administer litmus tests to things as labyrinthine as love and affection.

My friends who adore you:

....

....

....

....

....

....

Everyone is a hypocrite.
Hypocrisy is not the blanket failure it's made out to be; we all act in ways that conflict with the image we want to reflect or the values we want to embody. Try not to pigeonhole people with expectations; be forgiving of this inconsistency, both in yourself and in others.

The qualities I value most in a friend:

....

....

....

....

....

....

....

Not everyone's going to like you, and that's just fine.

The key to being a good friend is:

....

....

....

....

....

Look for the good in people.
It really is a choice you have to make, how you frame people in your mind.
It's also a reminder to yourself about how you want to see the world.

When a friend made me feel loved:

....

....

....

....

....

Gently tell people you love when you are hurt or upset with them.
You owe this honesty to yourself and to them—you never know; they just might apologize.

How I stay in touch with friends:

....

....

....

....

....

....

....

 Friends should build you up, not knock you down.
Be a champion of others.

Advice from my friends to you:

....

....

....

....

....

....

Sometimes people just want to be heard.
So it is important to learn how to listen.

I hope you and I have a certain kind of friendship:

....

....

....

....

....

....

More prudent advice

....
....
....
....
....
....
....
....
....
....
....
....
....
....

On Love

What do you believe love is? Every person has their own threshold at which feelings evolve from affection to love. When a budding relationship suddenly bursts upon this new dawn, it can feel as if the sun is singeing your heart with radiant joy. It's a delicate and delicious line, the one separating love and pain. It can feel as if life itself is in the balance, that the whole world fades away as you lose yourself. I can't tell you what love means to you, how you will know it, or where to find it; I can only share my experiences in hopes that they may help guide you to your own definition. One thing I know for certain is that knowledge of how the heart works grows deeper with age, while love makes children of all of us: sweet, naive, and guileless. In these sparkling days of your infancy, you are surrounded by the deepest love I have ever known, and in turn, my deepest hope is that love may tantalize and surround you all the days of your life.

The love of my life:

....

....

....

....

....

Yes, marriage is a long haul, but the highs and lows are not uninteresting.

"I wonder if it's possible to have a love affair that lasts forever?"
—— **ANDY WARHOL**

I once had my heart broken:

....

....

....

....

....

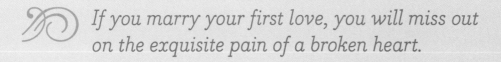 *If you marry your first love, you will miss out on the exquisite pain of a broken heart.*

You know you are in love when:

....

....

....

....

....

....

....

 If you rely on popular culture definitions of love, you will live in a state of constant disappointment.

Forget the love you see in screenplays and on sitcoms; your life is more tangled, more interesting, and, frankly, much longer than a movie.

You know someone loves you when:

....

....

....

....

When people show you who they really are, believe them.

The best medicine for a broken heart is:

....

....

....

....

Anything you chase after runs.

Things love can bring you:

....

....

....

....

....

You will know you're in love when you give the best bits away without thinking.

The best piece of chicken, the aisle seat, and a few hours to sleep in on a lazy Sunday morning: When you find yourself offering up these little luxuries, you've found yourself in love.

Things it can't:

....

....

....

....

....

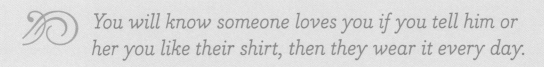

You will know someone loves you if you tell him or her you like their shirt, then they wear it every day.

The key to a healthy relationship:

....

....

....

....

People you love should feel safe when they're with you.

Things I've learned about making love last:

....

....

....

....

More prudent advice

....

....

....

....

....

....

....

....

....

....

....

....

....

....

On Kindness

Kindness takes many forms—compassion, generosity, benevolence, graciousness—but at its heart, to be kind is to free yourself from inward focus and connect with humanity. When you learn to access, reveal, and give the best parts of yourself to others, you unleash tiny droplets of hope that expand exponentially and infinitely. You will find that conjuring these gentle bubbles, whether of casual kindness or monumental sacrifice, is an act of humility with a personal reward—satisfaction. Learning to tune out your own fleeting desires and instead draw upon your reserves of kindness is a lifelong exploration of the way you interact with your community and exercise the power of the love in your heart. I want to help you realize the greater force of good that I see within you. Here are some things I've learned on my journey.

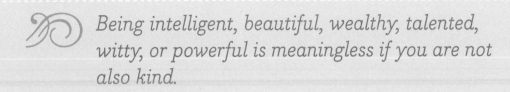

Being intelligent, beautiful, wealthy, talented, witty, or powerful is meaningless if you are not also kind.

One of my fondest memories of a kindness done for me as a child is:

....

....

....

....

....

....

And a kindness done for me as an adult:

....

....

....

....

....

....

Mind your manners.

As a child you may feel as though you're required to submit to an arbitrary set of rules: constantly told where to sit and what to say and which fork to use. I want you to understand the bigger reason for all this, even beyond conforming to social norms. As an adult you won't be afforded the same latitude you enjoy today to freely express your emotions. When the tide of your own passion is so high you're at a loss for how to behave, your manners will guide you. They are the tool you will use to maintain your dignity.

Be generous.
With your time, your money, your heart. If, on my best day, there was
a single lesson I could hope to impart to you, this would be it.

When I want to show my love, I tend to:

....

....

....

....

....

I had an opportunity to be kind, and I seized it:

....

....

....

....

....

⤵ Root for other people.

We all tend to envy other people's successes. It's not intentional; somewhere in our DNA it seems to be programmed that for every success for someone else, there is one less success for us. For every book published, there is one less book we will publish; for every baby had, there is one less baby for us to have. Of course, that is illogical. Fight off those thoughts; there is an unlimited amount of potential for everyone in this universe. Championing others is kind, and even more, it's a display of optimism that will seep into you and color your view of this life.

Cultivate the grace within you.
"Labor to keep alive in your breast that little spark of celestial fire called conscience."

— GEORGE WASHINGTON

I had an opportunity to be kind, and I squandered it, which I now regret:

....

....

....

....

....

....

 Every time you describe your good deed, you diminish it a little bit.
If you find yourself seeking credit for gestures of decency and goodwill, it is time to evaluate your intentions. Acknowledgment is not the real reward for kindness.

Emotions that will challenge your ability to be kind may include:

....

....

....

Every time you rescue someone else, you rescue yourself a little bit.

You will have occasion to save people: to throw a life preserver, to present an opportunity, to alter a destiny for the better. Seize these chances. Reflect your best, most giving characteristics. Rescue yourself from tedious inward focus: These are your opportunities, too.

You will find that diving into yourself and finding your inner reserve of warmth will help you face these challenges. Some ways I've coped with these feelings include:

....

....

....

....

....

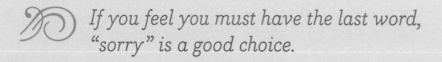

If you feel you must have the last word, "sorry" is a good choice.

More prudent advice

....
....
....
....
....
....
....
....
....
....

On Education

You will hear, throughout your life, that your education should be of utmost importance to you. Of course I agree, but the type of education I am advocating is not purely about intellect. It would pain me too greatly if I felt the need to explain to you why seeking to acquire information about your world is a valid endeavor; instead I want you to understand that *the desire to be educated* is the substance of a successful person. Our minds and our hearts are bottomless sieves, filtering the stimuli of daily life into articulate details that drip, drip, drip into our cores, seeping into our conscience and rippling through every choice we make. Whether you find your education in school, on the road, or in the folds of battered books, I want you to realize that it is the acceptance of what you don't know, and your desire to learn more about those mysteries, that will fill you up and make you whole. You are exclusively accountable only to yourself in this regard; you have only your self-discipline to guide you and your enthusiasm for the unknown to reward you. But reward you it will, as I have learned.

Questions I've explored:

....

....

....

....

....

I learned more from this than any other experience:

....

....

....

....

....

....

 You don't have to pretend you know something if you don't.
It's okay to just say, "I don't know." You can't know everything!

What I've learned about learning:

....

....

....

....

....

Where I went to school:

....

....

....

My favorite things about school:

....

....

....

....

....

College is a time to study your passions.

If I understood then what I know now—that college is the best opportunity to study everything and anything that sparks your interest, rather than just a way to prepare for a career—I would've approached it very differently. You will never again have the opportunity to spend such quality time immersed in pursuits that fascinate you. The day will come that you are immersed in one single vocation; college is not that day. Discover your interests and revel in the atmosphere of scholarly curiosity.

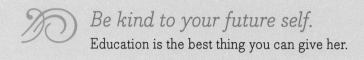

Be kind to your future self.
Education is the best thing you can give her.

Some challenges I faced in my education:

....

....

....

....

....

My favorite areas of study:

....

....

....

....

....

Do your homework.
But don't overwhelm yourself with too many classes and activities.
Take some time to enjoy being young.

What I hope you get out of school:

....
....
....
....
....

What I don't think school can teach you:

....
....
....
....
....

A lesson I learned that you will have to learn for yourself:

....

....

....

....

....

....

My hopes for your education:

....

....

....

....

....

....

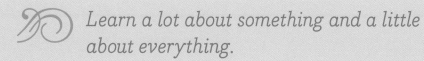 *Learn a lot about something and a little about everything.*

More prudent advice

....

....

....

....

....

....

....

....

....

....

....

....

....

....

On Travel

I encourage you to travel the world. Wanderlust is a hunger for knowledge—a thirst for understanding of your place in this world. Your journeys will feed it by forcing you to observe, navigate, decipher, and participate. You will learn from being homesick, being seasick, being lonely, and being awakened to the fact that your birth and location are glorious accidents. Then, when you return to the place where your journey began, you will find that your house looks familiar, though perhaps a little smaller than before. Take a moment to breathe it in, then step inside, take what you have gathered about people, places, and yourself, and use that collected knowledge to build yourself a home.

Where we have traveled together:

....

....

....

....

....

Whenever possible, take the train.

My favorite destinations:

....

....

....

....

....

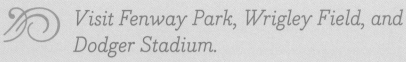

Visit Fenway Park, Wrigley Field, and Dodger Stadium.

There's nothing like a day at a legendary ballpark.

A travel experience that changed me:

....

....

....

....

....

....

....

There is nothing that clears the mind like a long walk in beautiful, unfamiliar mountains.

A travel experience that frightened me:

....

....

....

....

....

The Grand Canyon is as amazing as everyone says it is.

Something I couldn't have learned at home:

....

....

....

....

....

Travel light.

Baby girl, when you are a little bigger but still a young woman, all you need to begin your worldly adventures are some comfortable shoes, a warm jacket, toothpaste, and some books. And learning from my own experience, I guess I would supply you with an emergency credit card. Leave the blow dryer and checked baggage for business trips and traveling after you have a baby.

The most beautiful place I have seen:

....

....

....

....

....

Get in a boat and go out to sea.
Go far enough that you see only water on one endless horizon. Turn the engines off. Listen to the ocean. Grasp the magnitude of this planet.

Places I hope to take you to:

....

....

....

....

....

Places I hope you visit alone:

....

....

....

....

....

*Swim in warm waters, hike a snow-covered hillside,
lie in a spring meadow, and run in pouring rain.*

Don't travel without:

....

....

....

....

Thank those who offer you assistance in their native language.

Thank you, Danke, Merci, Gracias, Grazie, Gratia, Efharisto, Obrigado, Xie Xie, Arigato, Mamnoon, Tak, Cám ơn, Khawp khun, Dakujem, Toda, Köszönöm, Mahalo, Mesi.

More prudent advice

....

....

....

....

....

....

....

....

....

On Seeing the Beauty Everywhere

I encourage you to make time in your life for illumination and reflection. Practice using your senses, as well as your mind, to take notice of tangible details (flickering holiday lights, humming lawn mowers) that flesh out a particular moment, and abstract concepts (loss, karma) that help you make sense of what has transpired. Consider what is most beautiful and good in this world. Take an active interest in arts, letters, and nature while cultivating patience and your ability to observe and contemplate. Let your chest fill with love until it feels as though your heart could explode, then make note of what inspired you, so you may always remember the bounty and beauty with which you have been blessed. Our world is awash in wonder.

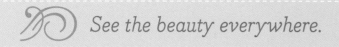 *See the beauty everywhere.*

Some things that have inspired me:

Poetry:

....

....

....

....

....

Music:

....

....

....

....

....

Quotes:

....

....

....

....

....

Artwork:

....

....

....

....

Scenery:

....

....

....

....

....

My visual inspiration board

On Finding Your Passion

What is the purpose of your life? I do not know the answer: It is something you must discover for yourself. But I can tell you that your purpose is not to acquire many beautiful things, to elevate your own comfort above the needs of others, or to constantly seek gratification in everything you do. If you can free yourself from the trap of self-interest and perceive your life and your actions as a type of service to other people, you will find a greater meaning in the activities you do every day. Experimenting with many creative outlets, careers, and even personalities as you seek to discover your passion is expected, and many missteps will be forgiven (that's what your teenage years are for). But knowing that you are seeking a reason for being and a way to service others that awakens your heart is what will keep you on a positive path toward a fulfilling life. When you identify the place where your natural talents, your practiced skills, and your purpose collide, you will have found your passion. This is the great expedition we are all on, and I want you to savor every step of your journey.

My great passions:

....

....

....

You will get good at anything you practice.
Everything gets easier the more you do it, good or bad, so choose your
habits wisely.

The purpose I have found:

....

....

....

The emotions I feel when engaged in pursuit of my passions:

....

....

....

....

Pursue more than just the things you are good at.

You will be told at a young age what your talents are. Enjoy the compliments, but don't accept them at face value. You don't want to walk a narrow path; attempt things you aren't comfortable with and uncover skills or proclivities you didn't know you possessed.

Pride can sneak up on you.
While I want you to enjoy self-esteem resulting from your successes,
it's important to keep feelings of your own merit and superiority in check.
A bloated sense of self-importance will stunt your growth: You won't
achieve much if you feel you're already so accomplished.

When I was young I loved to:

....

....

....

....

....

....

 No one is good at everything.
But everyone is good at something.

As an adult I love to:

....

....

....

....

....

Think about the way you spend your free time; read the clues.

"Many men go fishing all of their lives without knowing that it is not fish they are after."

— **HENRY DAVID THOREAU**

Things you are passionate about as a child:

....

....

....

....

....

Indulge.

Live a rich life textured with little extravagances. Eat the hot fudge brownie, buy the handmade dhurrie rug, lie in your flannel sheets all Sunday afternoon. Just remember that indulgence by definition is temporary gratification of a whim. Do it more than once in a while, and you're just a hedonist.

I suspect you will enjoy:

....

....

....

....

....

....

 It's true that some things are worth fighting for.

But I can't tell you what they are, little girl. Only you know that.

Discover your purpose and be fearless in pursuing it.

"A ship in harbor is safe, but that is not what ships are built for."

— **JOHN A. SHEDD**

More prudent advice

On Work

You are going to have to take care of yourself one day; there's no way around it. That means you will have to earn money, which in turns means you'll have to get a job, do it reasonably well, and collect a paycheck. This is a natural extension of the expanding responsibilities that accumulate as we age. You will work around the house, you will work on your education, and one day you will work for your livelihood. Your career may be a stressful or fulfilling aspect of your life, or some combination thereof, and not just financially. We all spend a significant portion of our time working, so we must make peace with our jobs. You don't need to love what you do to find serenity; you need only do it with integrity and grace. I have learned this lesson many times over and ask you to indulge me as I share that wisdom with you.

Some jobs I've enjoyed:

....

....

....

....

....

....

....

Some jobs I succeeded at:

....

....

....

....

....

....

....

Take pride in your work.

People will repeatedly tell you that to be truly happy, you must find a job that you love. I sincerely hope that you do. But in case you have to take a less-than-ideal position to pay the bills, there are some things you should know. Avoid any job that you find morally objectionable—you can't reconcile your values with tasks you find repugnant. But you can earn rewards from a job that you find only mildly tolerable. When you are presented with a challenge and use your skills to meet it, you will feel accomplished, regardless of the task. That feeling is universally valid and undeniably admirable; embracing it will make work a more rewarding experience in the day to day, even if it doesn't feed your soul.

Some jobs I've failed at:

....

....

....

....

Keep closing the divide.

I grew up knowing that as a woman, I was privileged with more opportunities than my mother had. I feel confident you will find circumstances even more favorable when you consider your career. Regardless of what calling you choose, please remember what our grandmothers worked for, and keep that legacy close to your heart.

What I learned from those failures:

....

....

....

....

....

When it comes to work (and most things), it is better to arrive fifteen minutes early than to arrive late.

The career I wish I had:

....

....

....

....

....

 Get the assistant on your team.

In business it always helps to befriend the executive assistant; he or she holds a lot of sway behind the scenes. Make sure the assistant who orders lunch for your conference gets a plate of food, include him or her in as many business decisions as reasonably possible, and remember his or her birthday. These are kind gestures with obvious benefits: If the assistant likes you, chances are, the boss will like you.

Dress appropriately for work.

Whatever your job is, choose clothes that are correct for that workplace; attire that is safe, clean, and (at most workplaces) free of cleavage. You might feel as if your clothes are an expression of who you are, and you want to be that person even at work. But I have found that "who you are" is often also someone who wants a promotion and a raise, and that doesn't happen if your clothing is distracting. It isn't about being pretty or what brands you wear or which skirt best reflects your inner self, it's just about taking the focus off your clothes and onto your work. If you aren't sure, look at the way your boss dresses and take a similar approach.

How I chose my career:

....
....
....
....
....

The hardest things about work:

....
....
....
....
....

Some tips that have helped me succeed:

....
....
....
....

Make peace with your work.

"Work is love made visible.

And if you cannot work with love but only with distaste, it is better that you should leave your work and sit at the gate of the temple and take alms of those who work with joy."

— **KAHLIL GIBRAN**

More prudent advice

On Politics

We belong to many levels of community, starting here at home with our family, then extending to our friends, perhaps our schools, eventually to our workplaces, our cities, our countries, and finally enveloping this planet we have been thrust upon. Members of these communities, you included, are charged with making collective decisions about great questions of justice and society. At times, the performance of politics can feel like a game of cards, a vulgar undertaking where everyone screams and no one is heard. Do not let this dissuade you from participation. Diplomatic engagement in affairs of state is a representation of your values, morals, and ethics in the most palpable, actionable sense. I look forward to intense and friendly debate of your viewpoint on justice and the greater good, but for now I can only share my thoughts on how government should serve the people, as well as our roles and responsibility to society, in hopes that they might inspire you to conscientious inner dialogue.

The system of government under which we live:

....

....

....

....

....

....

....

The greatest successes of our current system:

....

....

....

....

....

....

....

The failings that trouble me most:

....

....

....

....

....

Advocate for the causes you believe in.

The current administration and my thoughts on it:

....

....

....

....

....

....

....

What has changed during my lifetime:

....

....

....

....

....

....

....

What I hope will change during yours:

....

....

....

....

....

....

....

Acknowledge inequity.

Thomas Jefferson wrote in the Declaration of Independence, "All men are created equal." Today, we interpret "men" to mean "people," but at that time "men" was not intended to be inclusive of women, or even of men who were not white. Inequity existed two hundred years ago, and it still exists today. Don't let anyone tell you that everyone gets a fair shot. Be sympathetic to the disadvantaged and work hard to include them.

A politician I admire:

....

....

....

....

Politics truly can be a noble profession.
"Genuine politics—even politics worthy of the name—the only politics
I am willing to devote myself to—is simply a matter of serving those
around us: serving the community and serving those who will come after
us. Its deepest roots are moral because it is a responsibility expressed
through action, to and for the whole."
— VÁCLAV HAVEL

The responsibility of government:

....

....

....

....

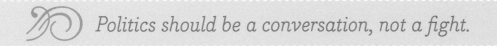 *Politics should be a conversation, not a fight.*

Questions government should not try to answer:

....

....

....

....

A cause that is dear to my heart:

....

....

....

....

What I hope you take away from this advice:

....

....

....

....

Understand the difference between values, morals, and ethics.

Values are the rules of right and wrong that live at the core of each person. Values are hard to trace and are instilled at a young age; your values are my responsibility. Morals are your purposeful ideals about bad and good; these are affected by your community as well as by your values. Ethics are a formal system of morals adopted by a group, a code you have agreed on in order to participate in that community. Each builds upon the former. It is important to evaluate these principles in yourself and others, to understand what you believe and where your beliefs fit in the spectrum of society. To be virtuous, you must be able to recognize virtue; to see virtue, you must consider what is virtuous.

You are not a party of one.

This world is not as solitary as you may imagine. If you do not have a voice, there is someone who speaks for you. If you have a voice and do not speak up, someone who needs your aid goes unheard.

More prudent advice

....

....

....

....

....

....

....

....

....

....

On Gratitude

It is so shamefully easy to forget how fortunate we are, even while surrounded by a windfall of magnificence in the form of ripe tangerines, fuzzy dog noses, teensy baby teeth, good health, and delicious tuna noodle casseroles. So remind yourself. Reflect on your blessings and say your thanks. No matter what kind of day you have had, you are a fortunate girl in one way or another. Set aside time to fill your head with thoughts of how lucky you are. Express your gratitude for these gifts to others and to yourself, and you will experience them more fully and appreciate them more deeply. It's important to bring these thoughts to the front of your brain; it cements the little things that make life happy into one cohesive positive outlook. Here are some things I've learned about embracing and expressing thankfulness for all that we have been blessed with.

The great blessings of my life:

....

....

....

....

....

Little things that I am thankful for:

....

....

....

....

....

 Always send a thank-you note.
This has served your mother and grandmothers well for generations and
seems a fitting place to start.

I show my gratitude by:

....

....

....

I feel grace when I see:

....

....

....

You have a garden.

If you ever get sad that you don't have a garden of your own, remember that you have hundreds of beautiful gardens nearby and all over the world. Try to erase the language of "want" from your head. You have everything that you need.

A time I felt appreciated:

....

....

....

I am grateful to you for:

....

....

....

....

....

....

I cannot overstate the value of "please" and "thank you."

We are lucky because:

....

....

....

....

....

....

More prudent advice

....
....
....
....
....
....
....
....
....
....
....
....
....
....

On Pain

Grief, heartache, and sadness are the inescapable price we all end up paying, in one way or another, for the rewards of life, love, and joy. As a woman, and maybe even as a girl, you will be confronted with hurt and anguish that my instinct wants to shield you from, but my experience reminds me I cannot. The best service I can provide is to arm you with the confidence and perspective to see the pieces of your life adding up to a whole and to know that each difficult experience balances the others so that you may face these inevitable challenges with strength, grace, and the knowledge that your suffering is only temporary. Pain will change you; let it be for the better.

A physically painful experience I had was:

....

....

....

....

....

An emotionally painful experience I had was:

....

....

....

....

....

 People will fail.
The unfortunate reality is that people will fail you, and you will experience what broken trust does to relationships. I hope that as a consequence, you learn the true value of the faith people place in you. Be worthy of it.

Something I learned from this experience:

....

....

....

....

If love were enough, no one would ever die.
Yet death is inevitable. Mourning invites magical thinking; you may wonder what you might have done differently to alter what has happened, whether a person would still be alive if you had only loved better or more. Your love can't keep death at bay, my daughter. But it can comfort you. There is nothing more I can say about grieving; you just grieve.

If I could save you from any kind of pain it would be:

....

....

....

....

....

You reap what you sow.

I have always found this aphorism to be deeply touching. I don't believe it means you are responsible for all the good and evil you experience. Things will happen to you in this life that you do not deserve. I know there is random unkindness and pain that I won't be able to protect you from. But if you plant little seeds of goodness wherever you can, and you work to reflect light onto them, you will find that with the warmth of your effort and attention, they will reap abundant rewards. These rewards won't come wrapped in patterned paper, but they also won't disappear. If you neglect these opportunities, or if you use them to plant seeds of anger or disillusionment, you will regret it. Life can be unfair, but your deeds repay you in kind.

I want you to be prepared for life's inescapable hurts and trials, such as:

....

....

....

....

....

Your pain will subside.
And something more powerful will take its place. It helps to remember that.

Some healthy ways I've handled painful ordeals:

....

....

....

....

....

Some unhealthy ways I have coped with pain:

....

....

....

....

....

When it hurts so much you don't think you can take another minute, call your mom.
I kiss your ouchies now, and your pain is suddenly more manageable, like magic. I promise that when you're an adult, I'll do my best to wrap you in a similar kind of love.

I've caused others pain, and the episodes taught me:

....

....

....

....

More prudent advice

On Happiness

While I hope that your life is a happy one, rife with the giggles and beaming grins that come so naturally to you as a baby, I have come to understand that sadness and its sisters fear, loneliness, and pain also have their own important place in our growth. Forget this reality, and it's easy to let your search for happiness become characterized by a more damaging behavior: pleasure-seeking. The hunt for moments of euphoria invariably opens up a deep, black hole inside a person. Life becomes a constant quest for whatever might fill this hole: Desperate people try throwing anything in there—toys, clothes, alcohol, sex—but the hole will never be full enough. The mistake is thinking that happiness is a goal you're working toward: It's an endless, selfish, and ultimately pointless endeavor to live a life focused on making *you* feel good. Know that lasting contentment is a side effect of choosing well; it comes from knowing that you have been true to your spirit, cared for those you love, and been the architect of your own life, for better or worse. When you feel whole, happiness surrounds you. Find your joy within.

I feel happiest when:

....

....

....

....

....

When I'm down I like to:

....

....

....

....

....

Some actions that boost happiness:

....

....

....

....

....

You are the wellspring of your own hope.

No one (besides your mother) will be more invested in your emotional well-being than they are in their own. Joy is not something gifted to you by other people; it's an outlook on the world that you have to cultivate independent of friends and lovers. Daughter, if I could give it to you, I would, a million times over, but the truth is that you are singularly responsible for your own happiness.

Be where you are.

Try not to think about where you need to go next or where you just came from. This is more difficult than it sounds, but work at it. It's important for your head to be present in the place where your body is.

You always laugh when you:

....

....

....

....

....

Unless you're playing a game, there's no point in keeping score.

Running a tally of who gets what in life will only frustrate you and annoy everyone else. It serves no purpose; the way life's benefits and hindrances are doled out will never make any sense.

We smile when we:

....

....

....

....

Ride in the front car of a roller coaster at least once.

Things we enjoy doing together now:

....

....

....

....

You will want some things that you will not get.
You don't get everything you want in life. That's all there is to say about that.

Things I hope we will enjoy when you are older:

....

....

....

....

It's okay if some dreams don't come true.
I wanted to be a mermaid when I was a child.

Choices I've made that brought me happiness:

....

....

....

....

You can find happiness in many places.
Don't rely on just one thing or person to make you happy: It can't.

Mistakes I've made looking for happiness:

....

....

....

....

Two things that make everyone feel happy: the beach and sunshine.

What I've learned about being content:

....

....

....

....

....

....

More prudent advice

On Health

You only get one body, and it is inherently beautiful. You may be blessed with strength and vigor or challenged by physical hardships, but either way, you have some control over your own health. The key to good health is habit—the more you exercise and the more healthfully you eat, the more it becomes second nature to continue treating yourself well. Don't get too hung up on what your body looks like; focus on how it feels instead. Beauty and health are intimately intertwined. A strong, healthy body builds confidence: A confident woman is radiant. Here are some tips and good sense on wellness and beauty.

I describe my health as:

....

....

....

....

....

It is possible to be both pretty and smart.
They don't always go together, certainly, but one thing does not preclude the other. This goes for you and also for people you meet.

My favorite forms of exercise:

....

....

....

....

....

Coloring your hair is an ongoing commitment.

Think long and hard before you begin dyeing your hair—once you start, it's difficult to go back. A lot of upkeep is required to ensure your roots aren't showing and the color hasn't faded; a lot of energy is spent agonizing over the most flattering shade and complementary tone. One day you may realize that you've spent endless hours and countless dollars in the salon chair just trying to recapture the beautiful hair color you were born with.

Foods I choose for health reasons:

....

....

....

A few less healthy indulgences:

....

....

....

When you smile, you are radiant!
You are luminous and resplendent. You are rapturous and incandescent.

Some family health issues to be aware of:

....

....

....

....

....

You don't need to draw attention to your own beauty or intelligence.

If you're really all that good-looking or smart, other people will be pointing it out for you all the time.

My favorite feature:

....

....

....

....

My favorite feature of yours:

....

....

....

....

First remove your makeup, then pass out.

We share these characteristics:

....

....

....

Take care of your teeth.

This is an incredibly boring piece of advice, but tooth pain is terrible, and unattractive teeth lead people to believe you are uneducated. That's just how it is.

My beauty routine:

....

....

....

....

Sunblock always, tanning bed never.

A beauty faux pas I made when I was young:

....

....

....

....

Your beauty is not something you earned; appreciate it but maintain modesty and humility in regard to it. Few things are as unattractive as a pretty woman who flaunts her assets in a boastful manner. Few things are as sad as a pretty woman who believes her beauty defines her worth.

A woman is most beautiful when:

....

....

....

....

Avoid smoking cigarettes.
It is extremely difficult to stop, and it will reduce your quality of life,
especially when you are old.

More prudent advice

On Fashion

Dressing and accessorizing can seem like frivolous amusements, but frivolity is underrated. Have some fun with your attire—it's a way of expressing yourself that can make little moments in life seem that much more exciting. But it's also important to understand that, for better or worse, people will make assumptions about you based on your fashion choices. There is a time and place for everything, from platform heels to business suits. Understand a few rules of style and dressing, and you can enjoy experimenting with your fashion sense without getting wrapped up in it.

I would describe my style as:

....

....

....

....

....

Leggings are not pants.

My go-to outfit:

....

....

....

Have a little black dress.
One you can dress up or down so it's always appropriate; one that makes you feel beautiful whenever you wear it.

My famous fashion blunder:

....
....
....

When wearing a dress or skirt, the hem should be longer than the tips of your fingers when your arms hang straight at your sides.

Some looks I've experimented with:

....
....
....
....

There is "trendy" and there is "classic."
Choose classic 90 percent of the time.

A time my outfit made my day:

....

....

....

....

Everyone thinks they have fashion sense and are a good driver.
Just let them believe it.

The best accessory:

....

....

The coziest thing I own:

....

....

....

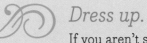
Dress up.
If you aren't sure what the occasion calls for, you'll feel better and make a better impression if you're overdressed.

You'll always look nice if:

....

....

....

Demure, dashing, dapper, and debonair are delightful ways to be described.

What fashion means to me:

....

....

....

....

More prudent advice

....

....

....

....

....

....

....

....

....

....

....

....

....

....

....

On Homemaking

You may think that, as a modern woman, homemaking is not a skill you will need to practice. I want you to understand why it is an art worth learning, for daughters as well as sons: You will all, one day, have homes of your own. Your home should be one of the greatest sources of comfort in your life. Treat it as a character in your story—give it attention and love—and it will bring you serenity. Ignore the banality of housekeeping (and it is so easy to put off for a more convenient time), and that chaos will seep into other areas of your life, altering the patterns of your day in ways more significant than dirty laundry and disorganized cupboards. Put things in their place, both in your mind and in your home. Organize in a way that suits you; treat belongings in a way that honors your investments; view cooking, cleaning, and entertaining as opportunities to feel harmony with others and a connection to your everyday self. Create a home that reflects your innermost ideals of a well-lived life, and that life will already be yours. Here are my thoughts on keeping a lovely and love-filled home.

About our home:

....

....

....

....

....

There's always room for one more at the table.
Just as there's boundless room inside your heart. Feeding people can be
a reflection of how much you love them. At least for mothers.

Fond memories of my childhood home:

....

....

....

....

....

Try to bring things into your home that you either need or love, and let the rest go.

The chores I enjoy:

....

....

....

....

 If you don't have the money to buy an extravagant gift for someone special, bake!

The chores I detest:

....

....

....

....

Use the good stuff.
There's no reason to hoard your possessions in anticipation of life's big events. Whip out your grandmother's jewelry, the fragile dishes, or your fanciest shoes to create little special occasions whenever you can.

Housework we do together:

....

....

....

....

....

Some tips on cleaning:

....

....

....

....

....

There is no substitute for baking soda.

Baking soda is a leavening agent that gives off carbon dioxide when it comes in contact with the acid in another ingredient. It fizzes and bubbles and creates the air pockets inside the baked good that make it light and fluffy, so if you're out of baking soda, head to the store or maybe ask a neighbor.

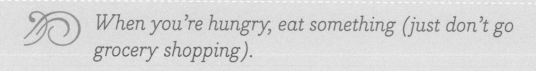

When you're hungry, eat something (just don't go grocery shopping).

Things I love to cook:

....

....

....

If you can, grow some of your own food.
Planting vegetables is good clear-your-head time. Then nurturing and harvesting them—with dirty hands and green all around you—is rewarding in a way that few things are.

The key to a memorable party:

....

....

....

Writing a list of tasks makes it easier to complete them.
Besides helping you remember what you need to do, there is something about checking things off a list that's so satisfying it's almost addictive.

Famous family recipes:

....

....

....

....

Food always tastes better when you share it with someone.

What I hope you remember most about your first home:

....

....

....

....

More prudent advice

On Being a Woman

You are my baby, soon to be a little girl, then a young lady, and finally a grown woman. What kind of woman you turn out to be is entirely in your own hands. You will have opportunities that your great-grandmothers could never have fathomed, and like them, you will face unexpected or unfair challenges because of your gender. Don't let anyone tell you that your sex is inconsequential. Your body, mind, and the landscape of your life are overwhelmingly influenced by your gender assignment and all the trappings that come with it. While it is not logical or helpful to generalize about the sexes, I do want to share some things I've learned about the unique challenges (and significant rewards) of growing up female.

My favorite thing about being a woman:

....

....

....

....

The size of your breasts truly does not matter.

When I was a girl, I loved:

....

....

....

....

As a girl, you love:

....

....

....

....

A woman can run a country (and not just be a princess).

See: Wu Zetian (China), Benazir Bhutto (Pakistan), Mary McAleese (Ireland), Ellen Johnson Sirleaf (Liberia), Angela Merkel (Germany), Golda Meir (Israel), Aung San Suu Kyi (Myanmar/Burma), Pratibha Patil (India), Gloria Arroyo (Philippines), Tarja Halonen (Finland), Michelle Bachelet (Chile), Helen Clark (New Zealand), Margaret Thatcher (Great Britain), Janet Jagan (Guyana).

Things that are considered girly that I enjoy:

....

....

....

....

Your period isn't gross.

Menstruation isn't something to be embarrassed about; it's just a personal experience that we discuss discreetly. You'll get more comfortable with it as you get older.

Things that are considered masculine that I've always loved:

....

....

....

....

> **Your sexuality is not a bargaining chip in the negotiation of life.**
> Don't trade on it; it is something specifically and only yours to explore and enjoy with someone you love. If you treat it as anything more or anything less, you're just gambling away your shot at true intimacy in pursuit of a false sense of self-worth.

It pains me when people assume women:

....

....

....

....

....

Remember that most fairy tales were written by men.

Some of the greatest writers of children's fables were male: The Brothers Grimm, Hans Christian Andersen, even Walt Disney. You are not a tiny princess awaiting rescue by a valiant man, a symbol of frailty and naïveté, or the punch line in a morality tale. The women in those stories were crafted by a different sex at a different time for a different audience; these days you slay the dragon yourself.

I hope you don't face this dilemma I faced because of our gender:

....

....

....

....

....

Sometimes you have to cry it out.
A good crying jag can be cathartic. It's a girl thing. Just don't do it at work.

A secret of the women in our family:

....

....

....

....

....

....

....

Balance is a sensation, not a goal.

"I've yet to be on a campus where most women weren't worrying about some aspect of combining marriage, children, and a career. I've yet to find one where many men were worrying about the same thing."
— **GLORIA STEINEM**

It is difficult to be a woman, because:

....

....

....

It is wonderful to be a woman, because:

....

....

....

....

 Compromise; don't sacrifice.

We are two women who:

....

....

....

....

More prudent advice

....

....

....

....

....

....

....

....

....

....

On Knowing Yourself

It is a mistake to believe you can ever really know yourself in a neat and tidy way. We are not such simple creatures; our only consistency is our propensity for change. Approaching your life as though it is a journey of self-discovery can lead to becoming an irritatingly self-absorbed person. Self-awareness, on the other hand, is an exceptional trait. Seeking to understand why you might feel the things you feel, choose the things you choose, and react the way you do is a valid and valuable investigation to undertake. Once you have a grasp on these characteristics, you will be released from the tedium of constant inward focus, free to go and live for yourself and others. So try to discern who you are, to accept your faults, and to know your strengths; then learn to be true to the woman you find inside. Just remember that overanalysis can breed insecurity: Work hard to strike a balance between curiosity and self-absorption. Maybe this advice will help you find yourself, so you can let yourself go.

My strengths:

....

....

....

....

....

My weaknesses:

....

....

....

....

....

My fears:

....

....

....

....

Live alone for a period of time.

I love living with you and our family; I also cherish the years I spent living alone. You shouldn't go from being someone's daughter to someone's wife to someone's mother without first being someone yourself. Living alone will allow you to discover who you are when no one is watching, what you need to get through a day, and ultimately that you are a capable, independent woman.

Ensure that the "bad" things you do are the result of your own choices.

You are doubtlessly going to engage in some unhealthful, unwise, or otherwise questionable behavior somewhere along the line; this is part of learning your limits and establishing your comfort zone. Please have enough self-awareness to at least make the choice to participate, rather than floating through life getting swept up in whatever trouble comes your way.

I learned more about myself from doing this one thing than anything else:

....

....

....

....

....

....

You can't base the big decisions in your life on what you think will make other people happy.

It never works anyway.

When you feel lost, it helps to:

....

....

....

....

....

....

When you feel bored, you learn:

....

....

....

....

....

....

When you feel shame, you learn:

....

....

....

....

When you feel joy, you learn:

....

....

....

....

 ## Sometimes you will feel alone.

It is a part of the human condition, and it is both inevitable and imperative that you experience this feeling. You will notice a variety of different responses to it throughout your lifetime: feelings like fear, relief, loneliness, desperation, even pleasure. All you can do is experience your solitude and observe your feelings about it.

What I think I already know about you:

....

....

....

....

....

....

....

What I hope you learn about yourself:

....

....

....

....

....

....

....

Do what you think is right.

I've shared with you this long list of advice: some lessons I've learned; some tips I've found helpful; some virtues I've tried to embody; some ideals I've failed to live up to; and some things I simply believe to be true. Know that I don't expect or desire you to live your life to the letter of my advice. My intentions are much more tender. I hope this list helps you discover your own way of living well, saves you from unneeded pain, orients you toward purpose, and rewards you with satisfaction. I know this is your life, daughter, and I trust you will live it with conviction and grace.

Do what you think is right.

More prudent advice

Things I Know to Be True

Ask anyone for the piece of wisdom they value most, and you will find no two answers are the same. There is so much learning to be had, and so much still to learn. I look forward to asking the same question of you one day and the many possibilities of what you might say. But while we wait for you to grow, I will share a few things that I simply believe to be true. Take them or leave them, but these are some facts of life from my perspective.

Magic is real.

....

....

....

....

Having good taste and being a good person are not
the same thing.

....

....

....

....

Some things are best saved for another conversation.
Stay on point, don't try to cram too much in, and realize when the conversation is over.

People can change, but you can't change them.

There's a science to everything.

. . . .

. . . .

. . . .

. . . .

The measure of your goodness is not the amount of love you receive.

It is the quality of the love you give to others. It takes a long time to learn this lesson, maybe more time than most of us have.

. . . .

. . . .

. . . .

. . . .

. . . .

More prudent advice